To: Sarah
on your 7th Birthday

Love from
Deborah

The author would like to thank Brian Gardiner of the Department of Zoology, Cambridge, and Peter Merrin of the Royal Society for the Protection of Birds for their help in vetting the accuracy of this book ; Hilary Abrahams, Veronica Barge and Maureen Galvani for their help with the illustrations, and Celia Henderson who helped to get the book ready for printing.

Swallowtail from egg to chrysalis

Dinosaur Publications

The National Trust
Second Country Book

by Althea

Dinosaur Publications Ltd Over Cambridge England

This book is mainly about insects and other invertebrates including butterflies and moths, the plants these animals feed on, and the birds that eat them.

Did you know that up to 500 invertebrates may live on an oak tree? Other trees and shrubs feed different kinds of insects so it's important to have lots of different types of plants and shrubs in our hedgerows.

Althea Braithwaite

The National Trust owns half a million acres of the most lovely countryside in England, Wales and Northern Ireland. Once under the Trust's inalienable protection this countryside cannot be altered, sold or developed, nor will hedges be removed nor trees felled.

Ownership by the National Trust is the safest way of preserving the flora and fauna of the countryside. But the National Trust is a charity independent of the government and it relies on its members for support.

There is a special membership for schools and for all those under 21. £10 a year entitles a school to a card which gives free access to thirty students and two staff into its historic buildings, gardens and nature reserves. If you are under 21 the subscription is only £1.50 a year and you receive the same privileges as do adult members.

If you would like more details about membership, write to The National Trust, 42 Queen Anne's Gate, London SW1H 9AS.

The National Trust needs your support.

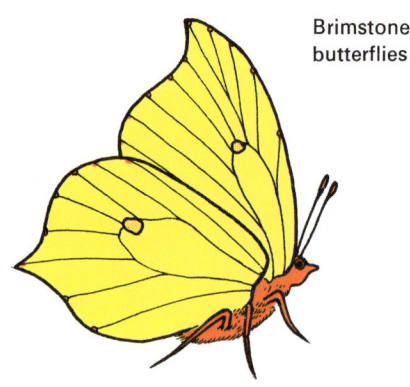

Brimstone
butterflies

Butterflies

Butterflies and moths both belong to the family of insects with scaly wings. The coloured patterns you see on their wings are made out of thousands of small scales, which rub off onto your fingers if you touch them. Each scale is really a tiny, flat bag on a stalk. Some of these are filled with colour, and others have a pattern on the surface, which reflects the light to make an iridescent colour.

Although butterflies and moths are so closely related, there are ways of telling them apart. Butterflies are usually brightly coloured, and only fly during the day. When resting, they sit with their wings closed above their bodies, showing only the duller coloured undersides of their wings. Their antennae, which they use to smell with, are always club-tipped, while a moth's antennae can be finely pointed or feathery.

The word 'butterfly' may have been invented to describe the bright yellow, butter-coloured male Brimstone butterfly pictured here.

The Brimstone is quite common in England and Wales, and can be seen flying along hedgerows and in woods.

The Brimstone is the first butterfly to be seen each year, and for many people it is a symbol of spring. The adult Brimstones hibernate amongst the leaves of ivy or other evergreens, or in sheds or outhouses, and come out on warm days in February or March.

Brimstone egg

Life Cycle of a Butterfly

All butterflies go through four different life stages. After they have mated the female searches for a plant to lay her eggs on. She nearly always chooses the sort of plant that the caterpillars will want to eat when they hatch out. She makes her choice very carefully, using the smell organs in her antennae, head and feet to find out if a plant is suitable. Butterfly eggs can be many different shapes, and usually have tiny raised patterns, which you can see quite well through a magnifying glass.

Brimstone caterpillar

After about a week, tiny caterpillars hatch out from the eggs. They start eating immediately, and hardly ever stop. In fact, many caterpillars eat so much that they increase their weight 3,000 times. As the caterpillar grows, its original skin becomes too small, and splits open, revealing a new skin underneath.

A caterpillar may grow four or five new skins, but about a month after it has hatched out, it sheds one last skin and becomes a chrysalis. The chrysalis is usually attached to a twig or leaf, and hangs there, quite still, sometimes looking like a rolled-up leaf itself.

Brimstone chrysalis

When the butterfly is ready the chrysalis splits open down the back and the butterfly struggles out. Its wings are damp and crumpled, so it climbs on to a leaf or twig and waits until they have dried and flattened out in the sun. Then it beats its wings and flies away for the very first time in its life. Its life may last for 10 days or 10 months, depending on its species, but adult butterflies don't grow at all after they have emerged from the chrysalis.

Brimstone butterfly

Swallowtail

The Swallowtail is the largest British butterfly, with a wing span of about 90 mm. It is a strong flier and is very handsome and distinctively marked. This butterfly is very rare now, and is only found in Wicken Fen and the Norfolk Broads. A few sometimes appear in Kent, but these are visitors from the European continent. The Swallowtail lays its eggs on the milk parsley plant which grows in marshy places.

When the caterpillar first hatches it is black and white and looks very much like a bird dropping. But when it is older it changes colour and is very handsome, being a bright green colour, with orange spots on bands of black.

It has an unusual 'Y' shaped organ at the back of its head which sticks up when the caterpillar is alarmed or upset. This organ is orange-coloured and sends out a smell like ripe pineapples to drive attackers away.

A Swallowtail chrysalis is fastened, head upwards, to the stem of a plant by a silken pad at its tail and silk threads round the upper part of its body. It usually spends the winter like this.

You can see the Swallowtail eggs, caterpillar and chrysalis on the title pages of this book.

Meadow Brown

The Meadow Brown used to be one of the commonest butterflies in Britain, but recently there are fewer of them about, and this might be because quite a lot of grassland has been destroyed. They like open fields and are usually seen there between June and September. Meadow Browns have a slow, weak flight, and often seem quite content to sit in the sun rather than fly.

Like all browns, these butterflies have very noticeable 'eye' spots on their wings. These can help to protect them, because if a bird attacks them, it will often go for the 'eyes' which are at the edges of the wings, and so the brown butterflies often escape with only a damaged wing.

Red Admiral

The Red Admiral is quite common in Britain, though it has to fly from North Africa and the South of Europe to get here. You may see it in gardens in England and it likes to feed on rotting fruit such as fallen plums or pears. It also likes buddleia and the flowers of the thistle and ivy. The butterflies arrive in Britain in May or June. The female lays her eggs singly on nettles and when the caterpillars hatch out, they make a tent out of leaves. When they pupate they do so inside a folded leaf, which is a good protection from birds and other enemies. Very few Red Admirals live through the cold British winter, although they sometimes do try to find a warm or sheltered spot to hibernate.

Comma

The Comma is easy to recognise because of the tattered looking edges of its wings, and because of the white 'comma' markings on the underside of its hind wings. It lives in woods, parks and gardens and is usually found in Southern England and Wales.

There are two generations of this butterfly each year, but the first generation only lives for the summer. Adult butterflies of the second generation hibernate in October, clinging to a twig or branch. The dull colouring of their underwings and their ragged shape help to protect them during their hibernation, by making them look like dead leaves.

Common Blue

Most blue butterflies are found in areas with a chalky soil, but the Common Blue can be found in grasslands all over the country. During the day, Common Blues can be seen flying quickly over the meadows, but in the evenings, they gather together amongst the grass stems and rest there, head downwards.

The caterpillars eat birds-foot trefoil. There are two generations each year, and the caterpillars of the second generation hibernate for the winter. In April they wake and spin themselves loose silk cocoons among the leaves of the birds-foot trefoil. Then they turn into chrysalises and each chrysalis rests in its cocoon until the adult butterfly is ready to emerge.

male

female

Adonis Blue

The male Adonis Blue is the most brightly coloured of the British blue butterflies, but the female is mainly brown. They live in the chalk down areas of Southern England and the caterpillars eat horse shoe vetch.

There are two generations each year. The first one appears in May or June and the second in August or September. The second generation caterpillars attach themselves with silk threads to the underneath of the vetch leaves and hibernate for the winter. In the spring they crawl into cracks in the soil and turn into chrysalises.

The caterpillars of the blue butterflies look a bit like wood lice and they have a gland at the back of their necks which makes a sweet fluid. Ants like this sweet fluid, and sometimes 'milk' the caterpillars for it.

Orange Tip

The Orange-tip butterfly belongs to the family of white butterflies. It is very common throughout the whole of the British Isles and can be seen in May and June flying along country lanes and on the edges of woods. The male has very noticeable orange markings on the tips of his forewings. The underneath of the wings of the male and female look dappled green, but if you look closely the markings are actually a mixture of black and yellow spots. This is good camouflage for the butterfly when it rests on plants with its wings closed.

The female Orange-tip lays her eggs among the flowers of the garlic mustard, wild mustard and other wild plants belonging to the cabbage family. The eggs are bright orange and are placed upright on the flower stalks.

She has to make sure that the eggs are laid quite far apart from each other so that the caterpillars aren't likely to meet. If they do meet the larger caterpillars may eat their smaller brothers and sisters. The Orange-tip caterpillar pupates in the middle of summer and the adult emerges in the late spring.

Silver-washed Fritillary

This is the largest of the Fritillary butterflies and has a wing span of between 72 mm and 76 mm. It gets its name because the underside of the hind wings are streaked with silver. It mainly lives south of the Lake District in woodlands and a great many are found in the New Forest. The butterfly can be seen between July and September, when it feeds on bramble and thistle flowers. The female lays her eggs singly in crevices in the bark of a tree. This is unusual because most other kinds of butterfly lay their eggs on the plant which the caterpillars will eat. After the caterpillars have hatched out they eat their own eggshells and then go into hibernation. When spring comes they drop down from the trees and crawl off to look for dog violets to eat.

Peacock

This butterfly is easy to recognise because of the startling eye markings on its wings. When it is resting the eyes are hidden because the wings are folded together, but if it is disturbed the butterfly quickly opens its wings and displays the eyes. This usually frightens an attacking bird away, because it thinks it has disturbed quite a large animal.

During the winter they sleep in a hollow tree, an outbuilding, or some other sheltered place. In May they lay their eggs on stinging nettles, and when the black spiny caterpillars hatch out they live in groups in a web of silk. Later on the groups split up and the single caterpillars turn into chrysalises.

Painted Lady

The Painted Lady butterfly comes here every year from North Africa. It arrives in May or June and often looks very tattered after its terribly long journey. Soon after they arrive here the females lay their eggs one at a time on thistles or nettles.

The caterpillars hatch out during the summer and feed on these plants. They pupate hanging upside down from the underside of a leaf. The new butterflies come out in late summer and in October most of them fly South. Any that stay behind in this country die because of the cold.

The Painted Lady has a very graceful and swift flight and you can see it gliding for long distances with its wings stretched out.

White Admiral

The White Admiral is a member of the Fritillary family and has a strong graceful flight. It lives in woodlands in Southern England and one can see it flying around bramble blossoms in July and August. Its wings often look a bit tattered, because they get torn on the bramble thorns.

White Admirals lay their eggs on honeysuckle leaves in the shade. The caterpillars, which hatch out a week later, camouflage themselves by sticking bits of leaves on their backs. When autumn comes the caterpillars build a shelter by pulling the edges of a leaf together and tying it to a stem with a thread of silk.

They start feeding again in spring and they pupate in June.

Small Tortoiseshell

The Small Tortoiseshell butterfly is one of our prettiest butterflies. The top side of its wings is very colourful, but the underneath is dark and dull, so that the butterfly is difficult to see when it rests with its wings together.

The Small Tortoiseshell is found all over the British Isles and can often be seen resting on garden flowers, especially buddleia. The females lay their eggs in clusters on the underside of a nettle leaf When the caterpillars hatch out they weave silken webs among the leaves and live and feed together. Later they separate to turn into chrysalises, usually on a twig or a fence.

Marbled White

The Marbled White butterfly likes meadows, wasteland or any open country with long grass. It is found mainly in the South and West of England. In spite of its name, and the patches of white on its wings, this butterfly actually belongs to the family of brown butterflies.

The Marbled White is a rather unusual butterfly because it walks on only four of its six legs. When the female lays her eggs, she drops them at random while flying among the grass. The caterpillar hatches and only eats the shell of its egg before hibernating for the winter. When it wakes up in the spring it eats grass and in July it pupates on the ground among the grass roots.

Grizzled Skipper

Skippers are small butterflies which look a bit like moths because of their size and their hairy bodies. Their wings beat rapidly and they have a quick, darting flight.

The Grizzled Skipper is found in Southern England and Wales and you can see it between April and June, darting amongst the flowers. The female lays her eggs one at a time on the leaves of wild strawberries, brambles and wild raspberries. The caterpillar weaves the leaves of these plants together with silk to make itself a shelter in which to feed. It pupates at the base of the plant in a cocoon made from silk and leaves.

Gatekeeper or Hedge Brown

This butterfly has two names because of the way it behaves. It often flies along hedges where it feeds on bramble blossom and seems to spend some of its time flitting around gates. It is mostly found during July and August in England and Wales. The female Gatekeepers are larger and paler than the males. The caterpillars, which feed until winter, coming out at night to eat grass, hibernate before the cold sets in and then wake up and feed again until they pupate in June.

Flowering Shrubs

There are lots of different kinds of trees and flowering shrubs in our hedgerows. You can guess how old a hedge is by counting the number of different shrubs growing in it. The more varieties there are, the older the hedge is, and each kind of shrub represents roughly a hundred years. Hedges are very important nature reserves, because all sorts of animals, insects and birds live and feed there.

Honeysuckle

Honeysuckle wraps its strong stems clockwise around the stems of other plants. The White Admiral butterfly lays its eggs on Honeysuckle and the caterpillars squeeze themselves down the long tube of the flower so that they can drink the nectar at the bottom.

The sweet scent of the Honeysuckle grows stronger in the evening, and attracts Hawkmoths, which unroll their long hollow tongues to suck up the nectar. In the autumn, this plant bears dark red berries, which are eaten by birds.

Ivy

Ivy, unlike most other plants, flowers in the autumn and bears its berries in the spring. Many different kinds of insects such as wasps, flies, bees and butterflies, feed on the flowers. The nectar makes them feel drunk and drowsy, and if you shake the Ivy, some insects may tumble sleepily out of it. In spring, Blackbirds and Thrushes come to eat the purplish-black berries.

Bees

There are about 250 different kinds of bees in this country. Some of them live all by themselves, and others like to live with lots of other bees in groups called colonies. The best known of these are the Bumble Bee and the Honey Bee.

Bumble Bee

Only the queen Bumble Bees live through the winter. In the spring the queen makes a nest underground and lays about twelve eggs. She covers these with wax and sits on them until they hatch. Soon, grubs come out of the eggs, and she feeds them with a mixture of pollen and honey. In two or three weeks the grubs are fully grown and become the workers. Their job is then to help the queen build the nest, and to feed their younger brothers and sisters.

Honey Bee

Honey Bees are smaller than Bumble Bees. They were known in this country in Roman times. They usually live in wooden hives and are looked after by a bee-keeper. Sometimes a swarm of bees escapes and goes off to nest in a hollow tree somewhere.

Honey Bees stay together all the time. In the summer they are busy storing enough food to feed themselves during the winter. The queen bee lays one egg into each six-sided cell in the comb. The workers collect nectar and pollen and feed it to the larvae. The other bees eat it too.

Towards the end of May, when the hive gets overcrowded, the queen will fly off taking as many as 30,000 bees with her to start a new community. She leaves a new queen to look after the old hive. The bee-keeper waits until the swarm settle somewhere like the branch of a tree, then catches them in a box and takes them to a new hive. Queen bees may go on laying eggs each season for three or four years.

Honey Bees

Spider

Spiders are very useful because they eat lots of flies and other insect pests. They are not insects themselves, and the main difference between them and insects is that spiders have eight legs instead of six. They also have sharp poisoned fangs to capture their food, but British spiders don't hurt people. They can see well with their six or eight eyes. Their feelers, which are quite short, are called palps.

Spiders live in hedges and buildings, and they can all make silk. Some spiders make the silk into webs which they use to trap their food. Many, however, lie in wait and pounce on their prey.

Different kinds of spiders make different patterns of webs. The one shown in our picture is made by a garden spider. He can spin the whole web in less than an hour. The outside framework and the spokes of the wheel-like design are made of a strong double thread which hardens as soon as he spins it. The main spiral is sticky, so that when an insect flies into it he gets caught. The spider then rushes out from his hiding place to poison it. Sometimes he covers the insect with silk, and keeps it for later when he is hungry.

Spiders often lay as many as 200 to 300 eggs in the autumn, and carefully wrap them in a cocoon of silk. They disguise the ball of eggs by attaching pieces of dirt or leaves to it, and hide it in a sheltered place, like a hole in the bark of a tree. The heat from the sun makes the eggs hatch the following spring.

Wasp

Wasps live in nests which they make underground or in outbuildings or attics. Each nest has one queen wasp who lays all the eggs. The queen comes out of her winter sleep in the spring and builds the first cells of the nest herself. The cells are made of paper, which the queen makes by chewing up wood. To begin with the nest is about the size of a golf ball. She lays one egg in each cell and when the baby larvae hatch out, she feeds them on chewed-up caterpillars and insects. The larvae soon change into pupae and then into worker wasps.

The workers build the rest of the nest and help to feed and bring up the rest of the family. By the end of the summer the nest may be about the size of a football, with up to 5,000 workers living in it. It is only when all the eggs have been hatched and all the larvae fed, right at the end of the summer, that they have time to go off to find the honey and jam which they love to eat.

When winter comes all the wasps die except for the new queen wasps who have to find somewhere to sleep until the spring.

Earwig

The common earwig is easy to recognise by its reddish-brown colour and by the pincers at the end of its tail. Earwigs use these pincers for fighting each other. They like eating insects, as well as flower petals and fruit which has fallen from trees.

Earwigs have quite big wings, but they hardly ever use them. After mating, the male and female earwig hibernate together all through the winter in an underground cell. When spring comes the female earwig lays her eggs in the cell. When they hatch she looks after the young earwigs, which are called nymphs, until they grow up.

Centipede

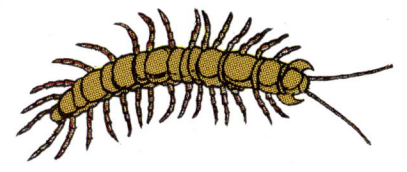

There are lots of different kinds of centipede living in this country, but not all of them have 100 legs, which is what the word centipede means. Some kinds have only 30 legs, while others have as many as 200.

They live in damp, dark places because they don't like the light and come out at night to catch their food. They are helpful to the gardener because they eat slugs and other garden pests, which they kill by using a pair of poisoned claws.

Millipede

The main difference between millipedes and centipedes is that millipedes have four legs on nearly every segment of their body, while centipedes have only two. Millipedes live in damp soil and eat plants or decaying leaves and wood.

Privet

Privet is often used to make garden hedges, but you can also find wild privet in hedgerows. The flowers have a sickly sweet scent which insects like very much, and many butterflies feed on them, including Red Admirals, Peacocks and Small Tortoiseshells. The larvae of the Privet Hawk Moth feed on privet leaves, too.

Dog Rose

The Dog Rose has flowers of deep pink to almost white. They are faintly scented and flower from June until August. In autumn, the red berries brighten up the bare hedges, and provide food for birds belonging to the Thrush family — including winter visitors like the Redwing and Fieldfare. Rosehips are full of vitamin C, and are used to make rosehip syrup and rosehip wine.

Blackbird

Female Blackbirds usually lay three, four or five eggs, and then sit on them to hatch them. When the baby birds hatch out, both parents help to feed them, and keep the nest clean by removing the babies' droppings. The young birds leave the nest when they are two weeks old, but the parents go on feeding them on the ground for another three weeks.

The same pairs of Blackbirds often meet again each spring, even though the male and female may have spent the winter apart. Each pair settles down on a territory and the female Blackbird builds a nest in the middle of it. The male goes out with her to look for nesting materials and he protects her from approaches by other Blackbirds.

Blackbirds like eating fruit such as raspberries and hawthorn berries, and they also hunt for insects and worms. When catching worms they stand very still, and watch and listen carefully. They can hear the worms moving under the ground, and as soon as they see the tip of a worm appear, they grab it with their beaks, drag it out, and gobble it up.

Thrush

The Song Thrush likes to eat snails as well as worms and insects. He usually has a special stone called an anvil stone and when he finds a snail he picks it up in his beak and beats it against the stone until the shell breaks. So if you find a stone with lots of broken snail shells nearby you can be pretty sure the stone belongs to a Thrush.

Song Thrushes nest quite early in the year, and have two or three families each year. They line their nests with rotten wood and dung to make them very water tight. After a rainstorm the Thrush sometimes comes back and finds the nest full of water. The female lays four or five shining blue eggs covered with black spots. She sits on the nest until they hatch and then both parents help to feed the hungry babies.

Cuckoo

Cuckoos come back to this country in the spring, after spending the winter in Africa. The cocks call 'cuckoo' to tell everyone they have arrived, and each year different people get excited and write to the newspapers claiming they have heard the first cuckoo.

A Cuckoo never builds a nest of its own. Instead, the hen uses all her energy searching for the nests of other birds such as Robins, Meadow-pipits, or Pied Wagtails in which she lays her eggs. Each Cuckoo hen seems to prefer the nest of one particular kind of bird and she tries to lay all her eggs, one in each nest, with one species. She has to find a nest where the eggs have only just been laid. Then, when both parents are away, she flies up and takes one of the eggs from the nest, and, cleverly balancing on the edge so as not to break the other eggs, she carefully lays one of her own into the nest.

A bird seeing a Cuckoo near its nest will fight to chase it away, but if a Cuckoo manages to lay her egg, the other bird will hatch it and look after the young Cuckoo afterwards. A baby Cuckoo is extremely greedy and soon grows very big. It will push the other babies out of the nest, and soon its new parents are left with only one enormous bird to bring up.

Yellowhammer

Yellowhammers belong to the Bunting family, and are sometimes called Yellow Buntings. They live in hedgerows and can often be heard singing a song which sounds like 'little-bit-of-bread-and-no-cheese'. They make their nests out of dry grasses low down in hedges or on the ground.

These birds are sometimes called 'Writing Larks' because their eggs are a dirty white colour and covered with dark lines and squiggles which look almost like writing. The hen birds have two families of between two and five babies which both parents help to feed.

In the summer Yellowhammers feed on insects and small animals. They also like blackberries and other fruits, and in winter they flock together with different birds to eat the grain they find in farmyards and stubble fields.

Goldfinch

The Goldfinch is very colourful and easy to recognise from the golden yellow bar on its black wings. This bar helps them to recognise each other when they fly together in flocks.

The female builds a small compact nest usually in the branches of a fruit tree. They have two families each year, and the female sits on the eggs to keep them warm, while the male brings her food. She has a brown back so she is difficult to see from above while she is sitting on the nest.

When the five or six babies hatch both parents are kept busy feeding them on insects and larvae. Later when they grow up their main food is seeds from thistles, knapweed, groundsel and other plants.

Wren

The Wren is one of the smallest British birds and because of its short, turned-up tail it is very easy to recognise. The cock Wren builds several different nests, which are ball-shaped with a small entrance hole in the side. The cock then finds a mate, and takes her round to see his nests. When she has chosen the one she likes best, she lines it with soft feathers to make it comfortable. Then she sits inside and lays at least five eggs. Some wrens have been known to lay as many as fourteen eggs.

After the babies hatch out, the parents are kept very busy feeding them and keeping the nest clean. When the young birds leave the nest, the parents go on caring for them, and they stay in their parents' territory until they are quite big.

In the winter when food is scarce, territories become less important to most birds. Sometimes lots of Wrens huddle together, sitting on top of each other in a small hole so that they keep warm during the cold weather – as many as fifty have been known to roost together in a single nesting box.

Bramble

Brambles send their long shoots sprawling all over some hedgerows. In summer, butterflies such as the Hedge Brown, Meadow Brown, White Admiral and Silver Washed Fritillary feed on the flowers. When the blackberries are ripe many different insects and birds like to eat them.

When the berries become mushy, Comma and Red Admiral butterflies suck up the juice. Spiders spin their webs among the leaves, to catch any unwary flies which are attracted to the fruit.

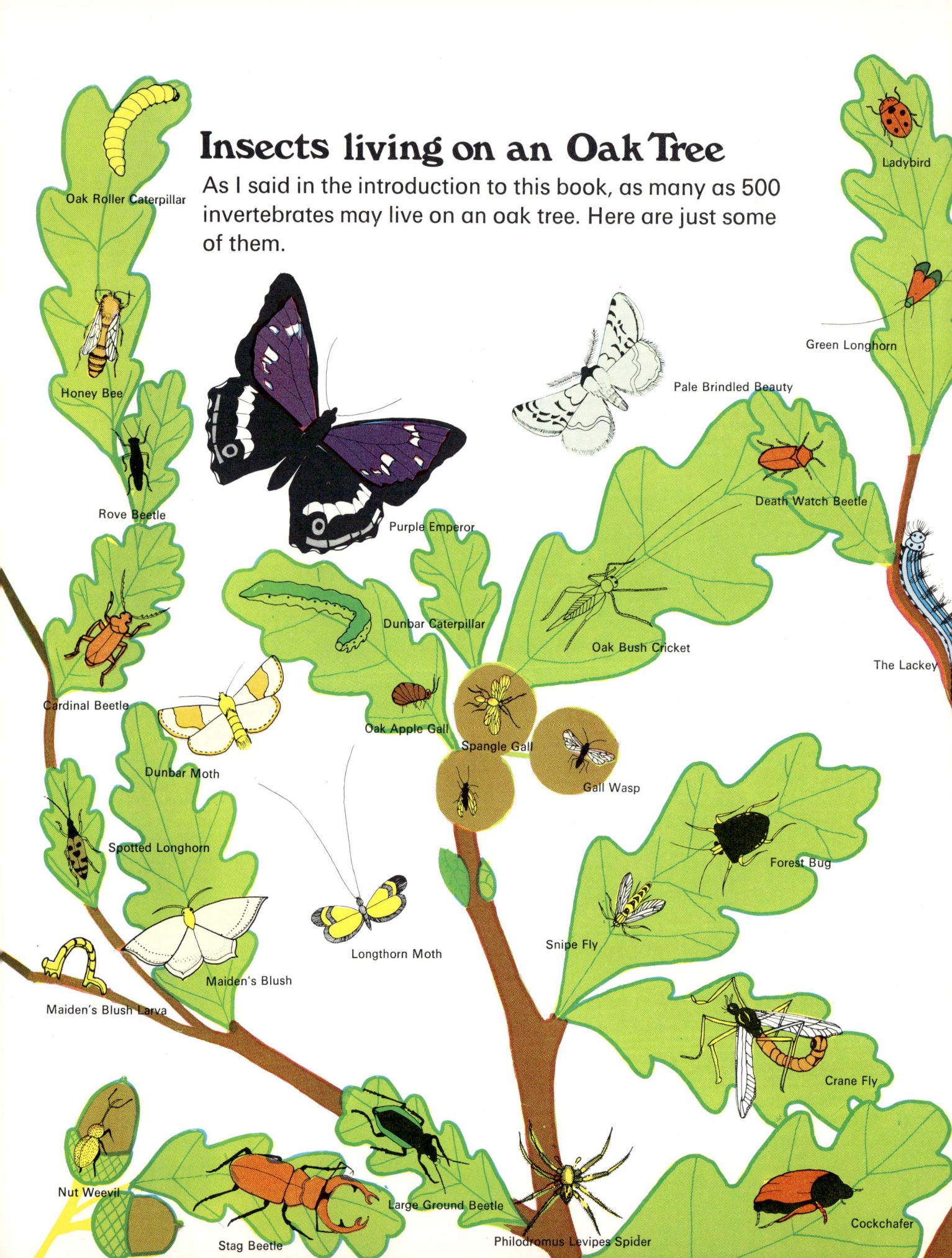

Insects living on an Oak Tree

As I said in the introduction to this book, as many as 500 invertebrates may live on an oak tree. Here are just some of them.

Oak Roller Caterpillar

Honey Bee

Rove Beetle

Cardinal Beetle

Dunbar Moth

Spotted Longhorn

Maiden's Blush Larva

Maiden's Blush

Nut Weevil

Stag Beetle

Large Ground Beetle

Philodromus Levipes Spider

Purple Emperor

Dunbar Caterpillar

Oak Apple Gall

Spangle Gall

Longthorn Moth

Gall Wasp

Snipe Fly

Pale Brindled Beauty

Death Watch Beetle

Oak Bush Cricket

The Lackey

Forest Bug

Crane Fly

Cockchafer

Ladybird

Green Longhorn

Lacewing

Red Necked Footman

Purple Hairstreak

Plant Bug

Plant Bug

Peppered Moth Larva

Peppered Moth

Buff Tip Larva

Lime Hawk Moth

Weevil

Bufftip

Vapourer

Lime Hawk Caterpillar

Pale Brindled Beauty – Wingless Female

Red Green Carpet Moth

Fan Bearing Wood Borer

Twig Cutting Weevil

Xysticus Ianro Spider

Puss Caterpillar

Pale Tussock Caterpillar

Oak Roller Moth

Four Spot Carrion

Swallowtail Moth

Tanner Beetle

Lobster Caterpillar

Leafhopper

Flowers

Sweet Violet

You can find tiny wild violets growing in all sorts of shady spots during the early spring. They are of different colours varying from deep purple to pure white, and the smell of the sweet violet is lovely. Their cousins, cultivated violets, are sometimes covered with sugar and used as cake decorations as well as being used to make perfumes.

The dark lines on the lower petal of the violet are called *honey guides* because they show bees where the nectar is, which they need to make honey.

Sweet Violet

Wood Violet

Marsh Violet

Celandine

Lesser celandines, which funnily enough, are not related to the greater celandines, come into flower at the same time as the violet. Growing in damp spots under shady trees, the plants spread very quickly. The flowers look very shiny and bright against their green leaves.

Lesser Celandine

Greater Celandine

Primrose

Primroses are another beautiful spring flower. They get their name from *primus* which, in Latin, means 'first.' At one time people used them to make wine, but you need large quantities of flower heads so it would be a shame to do this now.

Snowdrop

Aconite

Primrose

Cowslip

Cowslip flowers grow on the end of a long stalk about six to eight inches high. They flower a little later than primroses. They have a sweet smell and the bees are very fond of the nectar for making honey. Cowslip leaves look very like primrose leaves.
In the Middle Ages people thought that cowslips had marvellous powers as medicine. Ointment made from the flowers was supposed to cure all spots and wrinkles, and liquid medicine would end all other sorts of pains and sickness !

Cowslip

Buttercup

Yarrow

Foxglove

Sorrell

Mullein

Bindweed

Small bindweed is also called field convolvulus.
As it grows the whole plant twists itself around
other plants such as stalks of corn. It seems to
dislike curling round thick things like gate posts.
Its large flat bell-shaped flowers are either pink or
white. They come out in the sun, but even if the
sky only becomes overcast, they close up again.
Small bindweed begins to flower in June and
goes on flowering into the autumn.

Plantin

Mallow

Moths

It is usually easy to tell the difference between a moth and a butterfly. Unlike butterflies, moths mostly fly at night time. They don't have such brightly coloured wings as most butterflies and they often rest with their wings flat instead of closed together. Their antennae are either finely pointed or feathery. Very few moths live for more than a few weeks and many of them are quite tiny with a wing span of between 5 mm and 25 mm. There are large ones too, such as the great Death's Head Hawkmoth which is the largest British insect, with a wing span of about 140 mm.

Some moths have tiny bristles on their hind wings which catch on to a sort of loop on their front wings so that they can hook the wings together when they want to fly. Then the front and hind wings move as if they were just a single wing.

A moth's life, from egg to adult, is very like that of a butterfly, but unlike butterflies, many moth larvae spin a cocoon or bury themselves a few inches underground when they pupate.

Square Spot Rustic
The Square Spot Rustic is very common in most parts of Britain. They come to lighted windows at night and are often eaten by bats, who catch them as they fly. During the day, you are quite likely to find them resting behind curtains – even in big cities like London.

This is the sort of dull-coloured creature that most people think of when they talk about moths, but look on the next few pages and see some of the other fascinating moths there are.

Garden Tiger

The Garden Tiger Moth has a wingspan of between 65 mm and 75 mm and because of its size and bright colour, it is sometimes mistaken for a butterfly. The female lays her eggs in batches on the leaves of the plants the caterpillars like to eat, such as docks, dandelions and dead nettles. The caterpillars are hairy 'woolly bears'. The hairs are irritating and this stops all birds except cuckoos from eating them. When fully grown the caterpillars spin a cocoon out of a mixture of silk and their own hairs and pupate in vegetation on the ground.

The Garden Tiger flies at night, but it doesn't bother to hide during the day. It rests with its forewings folded over its hindwings. If it is frightened, it sticks out its antennae, unfolds its wings to show the bright red and black hindwings and raises a fringe of red hairs just behind its neck. If this doesn't frighten off an attacking bird, it should do, because it happens that the Garden Tiger is also poisonous. Some insects which are not really poisonous protect themselves by using the same bright colours.

Eyed Hawk Moth

The Eyed Hawk Moth is quite common in Southern England. It looks like a dead leaf when it is resting on a tree or fence, with its front wings folded over the hind ones. When it is disturbed it displays its hindwings, which have large blue eyespots, and this makes it look like the face of a large animal.

Death's Head Hawkmoth

This is the largest British moth, and also the largest insect found in this country. It can't survive the cold during the British winter and migrates here from the European continent every spring. It gets its name from the yellow markings on its back, which look very like a human skull.

When it is alarmed this moth makes a strange squeaking noise. To do this, it forces air out through its short proboscis, which is the hollow tongue it uses to suck nectar from flowers.

Puss Moth

The Puss Moth can be found in most parts of Britain. It has a thick, furry body, like a fluffy cat. The female lays her eggs on a willow tree, and the reddish colour of the eggs helps to disguise them as disease spots on the leaves.

The caterpillar is black when it hatches, but later turns green and purple, and looks like a leaf. When attacked, it waves its forked tail and spurts out formic acid. Then it rears its head and displays red markings and two black 'eye' spots, to frighten its attacker.

In September, when it is fully grown, the caterpillar crawls into a crevice in the bark of a tree. There it makes a very strong, hard cocoon from silk and pieces of chewed-up wood and inside this shelter, it turns into a pupa. The next spring the adult moth has to force its way out of the hard cocoon. It puts some caustic fluid on the inside of the cocoon, to soften it, and then it cuts a hole using part of the pupa case, which is still sticking to its head, as a knife.

Ruby Tiger

The Ruby Tiger is often seen in open woodland, heaths, moors and in marshy fields and grassy places. It flies mostly at night. The females lay large batches of eggs on heather, dock and dandelions. There are two generations, one in April to June and another in July to September.

The second generation of caterpillars hibernate, and then pupate early in the spring. The pupae, which are black with rings of yellow, lie in cocoons of brown silk among plants on the ground.

Burnet Moth

Burnet moths live in colonies, and fly around during the day. Their colours warn birds not to try to eat them, because like many brightly-coloured moths they have a nasty taste. If they are attacked by birds they frighten them off by producing a drop of yellow fluid containing prussic acid, which makes the birds feel sick.

The colour of the Burnet moth's wings varies according to the angle at which they reflect the light. This is because the scales on the moth's wing are not actually coloured, but have a raised pattern which reflects the light in such a way that they look green, blue or black according to how the light strikes them.

The female Burnet moth lays batches of yellow eggs on clover or birds' foot trefoil. The larvae make papery cocoons at the tops of grass stems.

There are seven different species of this moth. The Six Spot Burnet is the most common.

Red Underwing

The Red Underwing is one of the largest British moths, measuring up to 90 mm. It has beautiful red and black hindwings, which are kept hidden under its dull, brown forewings when it is resting. If it is disturbed, the moth flies off showing its red wings and the enemy chases the red markings. Suddenly, the moth settles on a branch, folds its wings, and because its coloured hindwings are hidden it seems to disappear.

The Red Underwing flies at night in August and September. The females lay their eggs singly on the bark of poplar or willow trees. The caterpillars eat at night, and make silk cocoons among the leaves.

Peppered Moth

The Peppered Moth feeds on oaks and other trees. Its wings are peppered with black spots. In industrial areas darker varieties of the Peppered Moth have appeared over recent years. The usual white and black marking is a good camouflage when the moth rests against a lichen covered tree trunk, but if the tree is blackened with soot, the moth is too easy to see and more likely to be eaten by birds. The darker moths are well hidden on blackened bark.

The Peppered Moth caterpillar has a long body with six pairs of legs at the front, two pairs of claspers at the back, and a long section in the middle with no legs at all. As the caterpillar moves, it loops this middle part of its body upwards, as if measuring the thing it is walking on.

Cinnabar

The Cinnabar Moth is found all over the British Isles except Northern Scotland. It can often be seen on waste ground in large cities, where ragwort grows. It flies at night and during the day. Both adults and caterpillars use bright colours as protection. The colours are to warn the birds and other enemies that they are not worth eating because of their nasty taste.

The female Cinnabar lays batches of yellow eggs on ragwort, groundsel or coltsfoot. Orange caterpillars with black bands hatch out and feed together in groups. As they feed, they strip all the leaves off these plants and this prevents ragwort from spreading as much as it would otherwise do.

Humming-bird Hawk Moth

The best place to look for the Humming-bird Hawk Moth is in parks and gardens where there are lots of flowers. This moth looks very like a humming bird as it hovers over a flower, quickly beating its wings. It likes sucking the nectar from honeysuckle, which has an especially strong scent at night.

In some years, there may be quite a lot of Humming-bird Hawk Moths in Britain, but in other years there are hardly any. They come from Southern Europe, and start arriving in June, often flying a hundred miles a day. Sometimes they breed here — laying their eggs on the bedstraw plant which is the caterpillar's food. When winter comes most of these moths die from the cold.

Elephant Hawk Moth

This moth flies at night time, and hovers over flowers, sucking up nectar through the long proboscis at the front of its head. It is called 'elephant' because the caterpillar, when it is disturbed, stretches its head and neck rather like an elephant's trunk. Then it draws back its head, and the neck swells up, displaying two large eye-spots to frighten off attackers.

During late summer, the caterpillars feed at night on rose-bay and great willow herb and fuschia. Rose-bay willow herb grows in empty spaces like demolition sites and railway cuttings, and the Elephant Hawk Moth can be found in most parts of England, Wales and Ireland, where this plant grows.

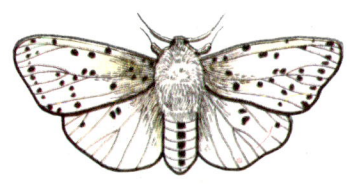

White Ermine

The forewings of the White Ermine moth are speckled, and look like an ermine cloak. It doesn't fly during the day, but can sometimes be seen in the daytime, resting on a tree or fence.

The caterpillars have long fur, which is dark brown or black, with a line of orange down the back. They particularly like dandelion and dock leaves to eat, but in September they leave their food plants, because they have an urge to hibernate. You can sometimes see them in groups on the march, looking for a comfortable place to spin their cocoons. They spend the winter among dead leaves, on the ground. In June the adult moth comes out.

Emperor

The Emperor moth has prominent eye-spots on its front and hind wings. The male flies during the day, but the female only flies at night. During the day, she sits among plants and gives out a scent which attracts the male. A male Emperor moth has large feathery antennae, which pick up the scent of any female looking for a mate, from as far away as half a mile. After mating, the female lays eggs on heather or brambles.

The Emperor is the only British member of the Silk Moth family — though its coarse brown silk can't be used for making material. The cocoon which the larva spins has a pointed end with a ring of spikes around it. The points of the spikes meet, but they open if pushed from inside, so that the caterpillar can get out but enemies can't get in.

The Drinker

The Drinker moth belongs to a family of moths called Eggars. The adults of the Eggar family have no proper mouths, but as the adult only lives for about a week it doesn't need to feed at all.

The Drinker lives all over Britain and is found in open country, mostly in damp, marshy places. The eggs are laid in groups on the stem of reeds, grass or sedge. The baby larvae like to drink dew and raindrops. They hibernate from October to April, then carry on feeding, and pupate in June. The pupa is wrapped in a long, brown, papery cocoon, which is fixed to the stem of a reed or grass.

Rose Bay Willow Herb

Corn Chamomile

Ladies Smock

Dandelion

The name *dandelion* means 'lion's teeth.'
Dandelions flower most of the year round and have
a nasty habit of growing in the middle of people's
lawns! They are very difficult to get rid of because
their exceptionally long root goes deep into the
ground and is difficult to dig out completely.

One name for the dandelion was 'pee-in-the-bed'
because if you picked a dandelion you were
supposed to wet your bed that night! The
seed-head is sometimes called a clock, because
people pretend that by blowing the clock and
counting until all the seeds have gone they can
tell the time. This is not very popular if you do it
near someone's lawn.

Dandelion roots are sometimes roasted and used as
coffee, or cooked and used as a vegetable, and
some people say the leaves are good in salad.

Red Campion

Shepherds Purse

Ragged Robin

Red and White Clover

Clover flowers are dark pink or white, and they smell beautiful. Bees are particularly fond of the nectar from clover for honey-making. Most clover leaves are made up of three leaflets, but it is supposed to be very lucky if you find one with four!

Farmers cultivate a different sort of clover for use as a cattle food. They also grow it to plough back into the earth, because the leaves of clover contain a lot of nitrogen which helps to improve the soil.

White Clover